I0089451

LEADING AND BLEEDING
WHILE GRIEVING,
BUT NOT DRIPPING

Dr. Laron Matthews PhD

Leading and Bleeding While Grieving But Not Dripping

© January 2026

By Dr. Laron Matthews, PhD

Published in the United States of America by

LMM Publishing

Scripture quotations marked (NIV) are taken from the Holy Bible, New International Version®, NIV®. Copyright © 1973, 1978, 1984, 2011 by Biblica, Inc.™ Used by permission of Zondervan. All rights reserved worldwide. www.zondervan.comThe "NIV" and "New International Version" are trademarks registered in the United States Patent and Trademark Office by Biblica, Inc.™

Scripture marked NKJV are taken from the New King James Version®. Copyright © 1982 by Thomas Nelson. Used by permission. All rights reserved

All rights reserved under International Copyright Law. Contents and/or cover may not be reproduced, distributed, or transmitted in any form or by any means or stored in a database or retrieval system, without the prior written consent of the publisher and/or authors.

ISBN: 978-1-945377-65-5

First Edition Printing

Printed in the United States of America

January 2026

DEDICATION

To everyone who has lost a mother. May your heart find peace, your faith remain steadfast, and your tears lead you toward healing.

ACKNOWLEDGMENTS

I extend heartfelt gratitude to everyone who has supported me throughout this journey of faith and healing. To my family, friends, and ministry partners — thank you for your prayers, patience, and encouragement. To those who are grieving, may this work remind you that your pain is not wasted. God sees every tear and redeems every broken place.

TABLE OF CONTENTS

INTRODUCTION

WHEN THE LEADER LOSES HIS ANCHOR

Grief has a strange way of showing up — not always when the casket closes or when the last prayer is said, but often in the quiet moments afterward. It's when the house is empty, the phone stops ringing, and the people who said "call me if you need anything" have gone back to their lives. That's when it hits you. The silence becomes loud, and the weight of what you've lost presses on your soul in ways words can't describe.

When my mother passed, it felt as if the world shifted under my feet. I was the seventh child of eighteen — one of many hearts she loved, prayed for, and carried through life. But even with all those siblings, her loss felt deeply personal. It wasn't just my mother who died; it was the woman who taught me how to endure, how to pray, and how to hold a family together when the storms came.

Yet in the days that followed her passing, I didn't get to fall apart. I couldn't. There was too much to do, too many others to hold, too many tears to catch that weren't my own. My father needed strength. My siblings needed leadership. The family needed order, and somehow, without asking for it, I became the one expected to keep it all together.

So, I led.

I organized.

I comforted.

And I bled.

I bled silently — not with visible wounds, but with a heart that ached behind a composed face. I showed up for everyone else while secretly wondering who would show up for me. I told others that God would make a way while questioning whether I truly believed it myself in that moment. My grief became a secret burden I carried under the armor of strength.

This book was born out of that tension — the space between leadership and loss, between being strong and being broken. It's for every person who has had to keep leading while their heart was falling apart. It's for those who have had to pray for others when they could barely whisper a prayer for themselves. It's for the ones who know what it means to be "bleeding but not dripping" — hurting deeply, yet refusing to let the pain spill onto those who depend on them.

As I reflect, I realize that not grieving was my way of surviving. But survival is not the same as healing. For years, I lived in that space of survival — busy enough to stay distracted, strong enough to be admired, but never still enough to truly feel. The truth is, when leaders don't grieve, they leak — in our health, in our relationships, in our emotions. God never called us to carry what He alone can heal.

In these pages, I will share my journey through loss — not as a story of despair, but as a testimony of grace. You'll see how God met me in the moments when my strength ran out. You'll hear how

I learned that tears are not weakness, they are worship. And you'll walk with me as I discovered that healing is not about forgetting who we lost, but about remembering who we are in Christ, even in the midst of pain.

This isn't just my story. It's a mirror for anyone who's ever had to keep functioning when their soul was fractured. My hope is that as you read, you'll find yourself somewhere in these words — and more importantly, you'll find freedom to grieve, to feel, and to heal.

So, to every leader, caregiver, mother, father, or sibling who's ever whispered, "I'm fine" while silently falling apart — this book is for you.

You can lead and still bleed.

You can grieve and still grow.

And through God's grace, you can heal — even if you never had the chance to cry.

CHAPTER 1

EIGHTEEN VOICES, ONE LOSS

Grief sounds different in a large family. It doesn't cry with one voice—it echoes through many. When you're the seventh child of eighteen, you learn early that silence can be louder than words and that love sometimes hides behind strong faces and unspoken pain.

When my mother passed, it felt as though the air was pulled out of our home. Eighteen hearts were left trying to find their rhythm again. Some of my siblings cried openly; others turned inward, pretending that strength would somehow keep them from drowning in the sorrow. My father, once the pillar of our family, sat quietly, lost in a grief that had no language.

And then there was me—the one everyone called strong, dependable, calm. The one who didn't crumble, who could handle the funeral arrangements, who could comfort others. I became the listener, the shoulder, the peacemaker. But deep down, I was bleeding too.

No one told me I couldn't grieve; it just seemed like I didn't have permission to. When you're surrounded by so much need, your own pain feels selfish. So, I buried my emotions under the weight of responsibility. Every day became about doing—making sure my father ate, checking on the younger ones, answering calls, keeping peace among siblings whose grief sometimes turned into anger.

But in the quiet moments—late at night when everyone else was asleep—I would lie awake and listen for her voice. I'd remember how her hands could calm any storm, how her prayers could shift the atmosphere in our home. I'd remember her laughter, her patience, her unwavering faith. And in that stillness, I'd whisper, "Mama, how do I do this without you?"

It wasn't that I didn't believe in God's plan. I did. I knew she was with Him, resting in eternal peace. But knowing that didn't make the ache any lighter. Faith tells you she's in a better place, but love reminds you she's not in yours.

Our family tried to move forward, each of us in our own way. Some turned to faith, others to distraction. A few avoided family gatherings altogether because the empty seat where she used to sit was just too much to bear. The dynamics shifted; the glue that once held us together was gone, and cracks began to show.

Arguments surfaced—over memories, belongings, and misunderstandings that grief magnified. I often found myself standing in the middle, trying to be the voice of reason, the calm in the chaos. But every peacemaker knows the secret cost of peacekeeping. It's the silent bleeding—smiling when you want to scream, forgiving when no one says sorry, and showing up when you'd rather hide.

I carried the weight of leadership, but no one saw the tears that fell in private. I'd wipe them away before sunrise, preparing myself to face another day of "being strong." But the truth is, strength can be deceiving. It can look like control on the outside and chaos on the inside.

One evening, I found an old photo of Mama. She was smiling—her eyes bright with the same light she carried in every season of life. I sat with that photo for hours. Something inside me broke that night, but not in a destructive way. It was the kind of breaking that begins to let light in. I realized I had been leading on empty, giving from a place of unhealed pain.

That was the beginning of my awakening. I began to see that leadership doesn't mean you don't hurt—it means you keep walking while you heal. It means admitting that even the strong need rest, even the faithful need comfort, and even the leaders need someone to lean on.

As I reflect on that season, I now understand that grief doesn't vanish when you avoid it; it waits patiently. It hides behind your busyness, your strength, your smiles—and it shows up in unexpected ways. Grief isn't an interruption to life; it's part of it. And if you don't face it, it will eventually find you.

In my family's story, I learned that God doesn't waste pain. Every tear, every sleepless night, every moment of "why" had purpose. It was shaping me—not to be perfect, but to be compassionate. To see others' pain even when they don't speak it. To understand that leadership isn't about having no scars; it's about leading with them.

Eighteen voices, one loss—but one God who can heal them all. The same God who carried my mother home was the same God who began to carry me through.

✦ Reflection for the Reader

- Who are you holding together while silently falling apart?

- What emotions have you buried under "being strong"?

- Ask God to show you where you're bleeding, even if you haven't been dripping. Healing begins with honest revelation and the courage to let Him touch what you've learned to hide.

CHAPTER 2

THE SILENT STORM

There's a kind of storm that doesn't make noise. It doesn't rattle windows or flood streets, but it can tear apart everything inside of you. I lived in that storm for years. To everyone else, I looked calm—functioning, composed, capable. But behind that calm was chaos.

My storm wasn't visible because I had learned how to hide it well. I had learned how to smile while breaking, how to encourage others while I was running on empty, and how to say "I'm okay" when my soul was silently screaming for help.

After Mama's death, I became an expert at managing other people's emotions. I knew what to say to comfort them, how to pray for them, and how to keep the peace. But when it came to my own emotions, I had no language. My heart was full, but my spirit was silent. I told myself that crying wouldn't change anything, that time would heal what tears couldn't. But time doesn't heal what you refuse to feel.

The truth was, I was afraid of my own emotions. I was afraid that if I started crying, I might never stop. I was afraid that if I opened the door to my grief, it would swallow me whole. So instead, I buried it. I smiled. I worked. I served. I led.

But grief has a way of finding cracks in your armor. It seeps through in subtle ways—fatigue that sleep can't fix, irritability that has no explanation, or a heaviness that lingers even when life seems fine. It shows up when you least expect it: in a song, a smell, a photograph. One day, I found myself crying in the grocery store because I saw a woman who looked like my mother. I didn't even know her, but her presence broke something open inside of me that I had kept sealed for too long.

That's when I realized—I wasn't just tired. I was wounded. I was leading others while quietly bleeding myself.

The silent storm inside me began to stir more violently. I started noticing how easily I was triggered by small things: disagreements, misunderstandings, even moments of quiet. Silence used to be my safe place; now it became my mirror. It forced me to face the emptiness I had been running from.

It was during one of those silent moments that I heard the gentle whisper of God:

"My child, you can't heal what you hide."

Those words hit me harder than any sermon ever could. I realized I had been performing strength instead of living it. I had been confusing emotional suppression with spiritual maturity. I had mistaken endurance for healing.

God began to teach me that real strength doesn't come from pretending the pain isn't there—it comes from surrendering it to Him. True healing begins when you stop managing your grief and start inviting God into it.

I began to pray differently—not for the pain to go away, but for the courage to face it. I asked God to help me sit with the ache instead of running from it. I started journaling, writing letters to my mother that she would never read, and prayers to God that came from a broken but honest heart.

Some nights, the tears flowed freely. Other nights, I sat in silence, letting my heart finally breathe. Healing didn't come all at once—it came in waves. Some days I felt peace, other days I felt the full weight of loss. But even in the waves, I could feel God's presence holding me steady.

In the silence, I learned something powerful: grief doesn't mean you've lost faith. It means you loved deeply. And love, even in loss, is sacred.

There were moments when I questioned why God allowed this. Why did He take her when we still needed her? Why did the one who held us together have to be the one we lost? But even in my questions, I could sense that God was not offended by my pain. He wasn't angry at my doubt. He was simply present—quietly, patiently, faithfully waiting for me to release what I had been carrying.

One evening, as I sat reflecting, I felt the Holy Spirit remind me of Psalm 34:18: "The Lord is close to the brokenhearted and saves those who are crushed in spirit."

That scripture became my lifeline. Every time I felt alone, I reminded myself that God was near—not just in my worship, but in my weeping.

The silent storm didn't end overnight. But I learned to stop fighting it. I learned to rest in the truth that even in the middle of pain, God was shaping me. He was using what hurt me to birth something holy in me—empathy, wisdom, and a deeper understanding of His comfort.

Sometimes, the storm inside you isn't meant to destroy you; it's meant to cleanse you. It washes away everything false—the masks, the pretending, the pressure to perform—and it brings you face to face with who you truly are without the titles or expectations.

I was still leading, but now I was learning to lead from a place of truth instead of pretense. The storm had stripped away my image of strength and replaced it with something far greater—authentic dependence on God.

And in that quiet surrender, I discovered that even in grief, there is grace.

☁ Reflection for the Reader

- Have you mistaken silence for strength?

- What emotions have you been afraid to feel or express?

- Pray this prayer:

"Lord, teach me to find You in my storm. Help me to stop hiding my hurt and trust You with what I can't control. Heal me in the places I've been afraid to look. In Jesus' name, amen."

CHAPTER 3

LEADING WHILE BLEEDING

There's a hidden weight that comes with being "the strong one." People depend on you. They look to you for answers, for comfort, for direction. But they rarely stop to ask, "Who carries you?"

After my mother passed, I stepped naturally into that role—the encourager, the decision-maker, the one who could pray others through their pain. It wasn't something I volunteered for; it was simply expected. I had always been the one people leaned on, and now, in our family's darkest hour, that expectation grew even heavier.

The problem was, I was bleeding. Quietly, invisibly, but steadily. My heart was raw, my spirit weary. I poured into others when my own cup was empty. I prayed for my family while silently wondering if God still heard my prayers. I smiled through sleepless nights and whispered scriptures to others while trying to believe them myself.

Leadership can be lonely, especially when your strength becomes your disguise. I wasn't just leading my family—I was leading through pain, through questions, through exhaustion. But I kept telling myself, "If I stop, who will hold them together?"

So I kept going.

Kept leading.

Kept serving.

And somewhere along the way, I began to confuse activity with healing. I thought that if I stayed busy enough—if I kept showing up, kept helping others, kept "doing the work"—maybe the pain would lessen. But pain that's ignored doesn't disappear; it deepens.

One Sunday, I remember standing in church, leading worship. The Spirit was moving powerfully that day—people were crying, lifting their hands, worshiping freely. But as I sang, tears started to roll down my face, not from joy, but from exhaustion. I wasn't just singing to God; I was crying out to Him. Every note carried a weight that words couldn't express.

It was in that moment that the Holy Spirit whispered something to my heart:

"You're ministering from your wound, not from your well."

Those words pierced me. They revealed a truth I had been avoiding: I had been giving from pain instead of presence. My leadership had become survival. I was helping others heal from the very place I refused to let God touch in me.

I realized that God wasn't asking me to stop leading; He was asking me to lead differently—to lead from surrender instead of striving, from brokenness instead of burnout. True leadership isn't about never bleeding; it's about trusting God to bind your wounds as you walk.

In that season, I started to learn the balance between pouring out and being poured into. I had to let go of the belief that needing help made me weak. I began to open up to trusted people who could pray for me instead of me always praying for everyone else. I allowed myself to sit in God's presence without a script, without performance, just raw and honest.

I remember one prayer in particular that changed everything. I told God, "I can't keep leading like this. I'm tired of pretending I'm okay when I'm not." And for the first time, I felt peace—not because everything was fixed, but because I finally told the truth.

That's when I learned that strength isn't the absence of struggle; it's the courage to be real in the middle of it. Even Jesus bled while fulfilling His purpose. He didn't hide His pain; He used it to redeem others. If the Son of God could lead while bleeding, then surely my wounds didn't disqualify me—they were part of my calling.

When you've been broken and still choose to serve, your ministry gains a different weight. You stop speaking at people and start speaking to them. Your empathy deepens. Your discernment sharpens. You begin to recognize pain in others because you've seen it in yourself.

Over time, God began to show me that leadership is not about perfection, but about dependence. It's not about being the answer; it's about pointing others to the One who is. My bleeding didn't mean I was unfit to lead—it meant I was human. And in my humanity, God's grace showed up stronger than ever.

Leading while bleeding taught me that it's okay to limp, as long as you lean on God. It taught me that tears don't disqualify you from purpose—they prepare you for it. And it reminded me that leadership isn't about never falling; it's about learning to rise, again and again, through grace.

♥ Reflection for the Reader

- Have you ever felt pressured to lead while your heart was breaking?

- What burdens have you carried in silence, afraid others wouldn't understand?

- Ask God this simple question:

  "Lord, am I leading from my wound or from my well?"

Prayer:

Father, teach me to lead with humility, not just strength. Remind me that my pain doesn't disqualify me—it draws me closer to You. Heal me as I serve, and let my life be a testimony of grace that bleeds but never drips. In Jesus' name, amen.

CHAPTER 4

NOT DRIPPING — THE ART OF HOLDING IT TOGETHER

There's a difference between bleeding and dripping. Bleeding happens inside—it's quiet, hidden, often unseen. But dripping? That's when your pain starts spilling out where others can see it. And for a long time, I made it my mission not to drip.

I had convinced myself that strength meant composure. That if I cried in front of others, it would make them uncomfortable. That if I admitted I was struggling, it would shake the faith of those who looked up to me. So I became a master of appearance—always composed, always smiling, always "fine."

But being "fine" became a performance. I learned how to keep my voice steady when my heart was breaking, how to host family gatherings when all I wanted was silence, and how to show up at church with worship on my lips even when my soul felt numb. I wasn't lying—I was surviving.

People often told me, "You're so strong," but they never knew that behind closed doors, strength looked like tears on my pillow, whispered prayers in the dark, and moments of staring at the ceiling asking God, "When will this hurt stop?"

Holding it together became my identity. I didn't realize how heavy that mask had become until one day, God began to gently remove it.

When Strength Becomes a Shield

It started during a prayer meeting. I was there, leading as usual—calm, composed, spiritual. But halfway through, as we began to worship, a wave of emotion hit me so hard I could barely stand. I tried to fight it back, to push it down, to stay "in control." But this time, God wouldn't let me.

Tears came without permission, and I found myself on my knees. No words, no explanations—just release. And in that moment, I heard the Lord say,

"You don't have to hold it together for Me. I can handle your brokenness."

Those words broke something in me that years of composure never could. For the first time, I realized that strength is not the absence of tears—it's the willingness to bring those tears to God.

I had been holding my grief in one hand and my responsibilities in the other, trying to balance both without breaking. But God was inviting me to lay them both at His feet.

Holding it together might keep you functional, but it doesn't make you free. And God desires freedom more than performance.

The Hidden Cost of "I'm Fine"

When you refuse to process your pain, it leaks into every part of your life. I didn't notice it at first, but I started becoming distant— emotionally numb, easily irritated, quick to withdraw. My patience was thin, my joy was dim, and my peace felt temporary.

Grief, when ignored, disguises itself as strength but disguises itself as burnout, detachment, and weariness. I was operating in survival mode, mistaking numbness for healing.

But God never called us to manage pain—He called us to release it.

One night, I sat in my living room surrounded by silence. I felt the weight of years of "holding it together" pressing on my chest. And I prayed a simple but honest prayer:

"God, I'm tired of being strong."

And in the quiet that followed, I felt His presence fill the room like a warm blanket. I didn't hear thunder or see visions—just peace. And I knew that was Him saying, "Then let Me be strong for you."

That night, I realized that the art of not dripping isn't about control— it's about surrender. It's about learning when to stand and when to fall. When to lead and when to rest. When to speak and when to simply cry in the Father's arms.

God's Kind of Strength

The world teaches us to "keep it together," but the Kingdom teaches us to cast it off. Scripture reminds us in 1 Peter 5:7:

"Cast all your anxiety on Him, because He cares for you."

That verse became my lifeline. I started to understand that being held together doesn't mean doing it myself—it means letting God hold me.

Little by little, I stopped apologizing for my tears. I stopped hiding my humanity. I began to lead from authenticity, not performance. I learned that people aren't inspired by your perfection—they're inspired by your perseverance. They find hope not when you hide your scars, but when you show them what grace can do through them.

And something powerful happened when I started being real: others did too. My honesty gave others permission to exhale, to stop pretending, to begin their own healing.

That's when I saw the beauty in brokenness—the way God can take the very pieces you tried to hide and use them as instruments of healing for others.

Holding It Together vs. Being Held

The art of "not dripping" isn't about suppressing your pain—it's about trusting God enough to carry it. There's a holy strength in surrender, a quiet confidence that says, "I don't have to be in control; I just have to stay connected."

Yes, I was still bleeding, but I wasn't collapsing. I was still hurting, but I was no longer hiding. And in that space of honesty, I found a new kind of peace—the peace that comes when you stop pretending and start trusting.

So I keep leading, but differently now. Not with pressure, but with presence. Not from fear of falling apart, but from faith that even if I do, God can hold every piece.

● Reflection for the Reader

- Have you mistaken control for strength?

- What would happen if you let God see the parts of you you've been holding together for too long?

- Take a deep breath and pray this:

Prayer:

Heavenly Father, I've tried to hold everything together in my own strength. But today, I give You my pieces. Teach me to rest in You, to trust that You can hold what I cannot. Let my composure be replaced by Your peace, and my pressure by Your presence. In Jesus' name, amen.

CHAPTER 5

WHEN GRIEF BECOMES A MINISTRY

Pain changes you. It rearranges the way you see people, the way you listen, the way you pray. When you've walked through deep loss, your heart starts to recognize brokenness in others—even when they try to hide it behind a smile.

That's what began happening to me. What once felt like a curse started to look like a calling. My grief had become a ministry—not one I chose, but one God birthed out of my tears.

The Ministry You Don't Apply For

I didn't plan to minister through grief. I never prayed, "Lord, make me the one who comforts others who are hurting." But that's the thing about divine purpose—it often grows in the soil of your suffering.

At first, it started with quiet moments. Someone at church would lose a loved one, and I'd find myself drawn to them—not out of duty, but out of compassion. I didn't come with fancy words or scriptures; I came with presence. Because when you've been there, you know that silence can be more healing than speeches.

I would sit beside them, hold their hand, and sometimes just cry with them. And in those moments, I felt God whisper, "This is ministry."

It wasn't the kind of ministry that needed a microphone or a title. It was the ministry of empathy—the sacred ability to feel what someone else feels and to remind them that they're not alone.

That's when I realized: my grief had not disqualified me from serving God—it had qualified me in a new way.

The Power of Shared Pain

When my mother died, I thought I had lost everything I needed to give. But God showed me that what I lost in comfort, I gained in compassion.

People who had known me for years started opening up about their own pain. They saw in me not perfection, but identification. They saw that I wasn't speaking from theory—I was speaking from the trenches. And that gave them hope.

The same tears that once embarrassed me became tools of ministry. The same nights I thought I wouldn't survive became testimonies that encouraged others to hold on.

There's a strange beauty in shared sorrow. It connects people in ways that ease cannot. It teaches you that sometimes your greatest ministry isn't what you say—it's how you survive.

God's Redemption of Suffering

Romans 8:28 says, "And we know that all things work together for good to them that love God, to them who are the called according to His purpose."

For a long time, I didn't see how that verse could apply to my pain. How could losing my mother, the heart of our family, possibly work for good? But as the years passed, I began to see the threads of redemption weaving through the fabric of my grief.

God never wasted a single tear. Every moment of heartbreak became an ingredient in my healing and in the healing of others.

He showed me that ministry isn't just about preaching to the masses—it's about touching the one who's sitting in silence, wondering if God still sees them.

Grief taught me how to minister differently. It made me slower to judge, quicker to listen, and softer in my approach. I learned that sometimes, people don't need a verse—they need a voice that says, "I've been there too, and God brought me through."

The Gift Hidden in the Wound

There's something sacred about realizing that your wound carries wisdom. You begin to understand that what broke you wasn't meant to destroy you—it was meant to transform you.

I used to ask God, "Why me?" But now I ask, "Who can I help because it was me?"

When you reach that point, grief becomes a gift. Not because it was good, but because it produced good. It gave birth to something holy—a ministry that flows not from pride, but from pain that's been purified by God's grace.

I began to see my mother's legacy in every life touched through my story. Her prayers didn't die with her—they lived on through me. Her faith became the bridge that carried me from despair to destiny. And through that, I found peace.

From Mourning to Mission

One day, I was speaking at a women's gathering, sharing about loss and healing. Afterward, a woman came up to me with tears in her eyes. She said, "I thought I was the only one. But hearing you talk made me believe I can heal too."

In that moment, I understood my purpose. My grief had become my message. My tears had become my testimony. What once silenced me now gave me something to say.

When grief becomes a ministry, your pain turns into prophecy—it declares that God can resurrect joy from ashes and purpose from pain.

The Healing in Helping

I discovered that helping others heal was part of my own healing. Each conversation, each prayer, each hug became a step toward wholeness. God used the very thing that hurt me to heal me.

Now, I no longer see my story as something to hide; I see it as something to share. Because every time I tell it, I remind someone that God still restores, still redeems, and still resurrects.

Grief doesn't have to end in despair—it can end in destiny.

❦ Reflection for the Reader

- What pain has God been trying to turn into purpose in your life?

- Who might need your story right now?

- Ask God to reveal how your wounds can become wells of healing for others.

Prayer:

Father, thank You for turning my pain into purpose. Teach me how to serve from my scars, not my strength. Use my story to bring comfort to others, and let every tear I've cried become a seed of healing for someone else. In Jesus' name, amen.

CHAPTER 6

THE FATHER AND THE VOID

When Mama passed away, it felt like the heart of our family stopped beating. But as time went on, I realized that while I was grieving the loss of a mother, my father was grieving the loss of a lifelong companion.

They had built a world together—a rhythm of love, partnership, and shared faith that anchored our home. And when she left, that rhythm broke. The silence in the house was different after she was gone. It wasn't just quiet—it was hollow.

I remember watching my father sit in his favorite chair, staring into space as if waiting for her to walk through the door. He didn't talk much about how he felt; men of his generation rarely did. But his silence said more than words ever could.

At first, I tried to fill that silence—with conversations, with care, with presence. I would check on him constantly, make sure he had meals, keep the house in order. But no matter what I did, I couldn't fill the void she left behind.

And somewhere deep down, I began to feel resentment—not toward him, but toward the situation. I was angry that I had to be strong for everyone, including him. Angry that my grief had to wait while his took priority. Angry that the father I once looked to for strength now looked to me for stability.

But as I grew in understanding, God began to show me something I hadn't seen before: my father wasn't distant—he was drowning.

The Silent Pain of a Father

It's easy to forget that men grieve too, though they rarely show it the way we expect. My father's grief came out in short tempers, long silences, and restless nights. He didn't cry often, but I saw it in his eyes—the kind of pain that doesn't ask for help because it doesn't know how to.

He had spent his whole life being the protector, the provider, the leader. Losing Mama stripped him of the one person who saw his softness, who understood his fears, who prayed for him when no one else did.

And suddenly, the man I had always depended on was the one depending on me.

That shift was hard to accept. It forced me to grow in ways I wasn't ready for. I wanted to grieve with him, but instead, I found myself grieving for him. Watching him fade into quiet routines and long pauses made me realize that grief doesn't just take the person you love—it takes parts of you too.

The Weight of Unspoken Words

There were things I wished I could say to him—how much I missed her, how lost I felt without her prayers, how hard it was to be strong when my own heart was shattered. But every time I tried, the words caught in my throat.

Our conversations became practical: "Do you need anything from the store?" "Did you eat today?" "How are you feeling?"—though we both knew the real question we wanted to ask was, "How are you surviving?"

It took time—even—for me to understand that healing doesn't always come through talking. Sometimes it comes through presence. Through showing up even when words fail. Through quiet acts of love that say, "I see you. I understand. I'm here."

Over time, I realized that forgiveness wasn't just about releasing anger—it was about releasing expectations. I had to forgive my father for not grieving the way I wanted him to, and forgive myself for not being able to fix what was never mine to heal.

When God Steps Into the Void

One night, as I was praying for him, I heard the Lord say,

"You can't be his comforter. Only I can."

That truth broke me and freed me at the same time. I had been trying to play a role only God could fill. I wanted to be his strength, his encouragement, his healer—but God reminded me that He is the Father of all comfort.

I began to pray differently after that. Instead of asking God to change my father, I asked Him to cover him. I prayed that the same peace that was healing me would also reach him.

And slowly, I began to see subtle changes. He started talking more—about her, about their life together, about the memories that once brought pain but now brought smiles. I realized then that grief doesn't always end—it evolves. The pain doesn't vanish; it transforms into gratitude.

Lessons From a Father's Grief

My father's grief taught me something profound: love doesn't die when a person does—it shifts form. It becomes memory, legacy, reflection.

Through him, I saw what faithful love looks like when it has nowhere to go. I saw devotion that lingered long after the wedding vows ended. I saw faith that endured loss without understanding it.

And though he never said it out loud, his quiet endurance reminded me that sometimes, strength isn't loud—it's loyal.

God used that season to reconcile parts of our relationship that had been wounded for years. We began to talk more, pray more, and even laugh again. The void didn't close, but it became sacred ground—holy space where both of us learned to lean on God instead of each other.

The Healing That Flows Through Forgiveness

Forgiveness healed more than just my heart—it restored connection. I stopped expecting my father to be who he once was and started embracing who he was becoming.

And in that acceptance, I found peace.

Sometimes, healing looks like a hug after years of distance. Sometimes it's a prayer whispered through tears. And sometimes, it's simply sitting beside someone in silence, knowing that even without words, love remains.

❄ Reflection for the Reader

- Who in your family are you still holding expectations against?

- ' What unspoken pain might exist between you and them?

- Take time to pray this:

Prayer:

Father, help me to see others' pain the way You see it. Teach me to love without judgment and forgive without hesitation. Where there is distance, bring connection. Where there is silence, bring understanding. Heal the unspoken wounds in my family, and fill every void with Your presence. In Jesus' name, amen.

CHAPTER 7

FAITH IN THE MIDDLE OF THE FUNERAL

G rief doesn't ask for permission; it simply arrives. It interrupts your faith, your rhythm, your sense of control. I learned this truth standing in a church filled with flowers, tears, and memories — the day we laid my mother to rest.

I had stood in that same sanctuary many times before. I had sung, prayed, and shouted praises in that very place. But that day felt different. The air was heavy, the music somber, the presence of death undeniable. I remember gripping the edge of the pew as the choir sang her favorite hymn. My heart believed she was in a better place, but my flesh whispered, "She should still be here."

Faith felt complicated in that moment. It wasn't gone—it was just buried beneath layers of pain and confusion.

When Faith Meets Reality

I had always been taught that faith means trusting God no matter what. But I found myself wondering, What happens when "no matter what" hurts this much?

I believed God could heal. I had prayed for healing. We had fasted, cried out, and stood on His promises. And yet, the healing I had hoped for didn't come on this side of eternity.

That realization shook me. It didn't make me doubt God's existence, but it did make me question His decisions. How could the same God who raised Lazarus from the dead take the one person who held our family together?

In that space of questioning, I felt torn between belief and bitterness. My mind knew the Scriptures, but my heart was still raw.

One night after the funeral, I sat in the quiet, Bible open but unread. Through tears I said, "God, I know You're good, but this doesn't feel good."

And in the stillness, I felt the Lord whisper, "Faith is not about what feels good; it's about Who I am even when it doesn't."

That changed everything.

The Kind of Faith That Doesn't Need Answers

Faith in the middle of the funeral isn't loud. It doesn't always shout hallelujah or dance through pain. Sometimes it just sits there— broken, quiet, and barely breathing—but still believing.

I learned that day that faith doesn't always move mountains; sometimes it just helps you stand beside one.

I didn't have all the answers, but I had one truth I could hold onto: God was still God.

Even when I couldn't trace His hand, I could trust His heart.

That became my anchor. I stopped trying to figure out the "why" and started asking God to show me the "who"—who He was in the middle of it, who He was becoming to me through it.

And slowly, faith began to rebuild itself—not through miracles, but through moments.

Moments when peace came out of nowhere.

Moments when I woke up and realized I hadn't cried that day.

Moments when laughter returned to the same lips that had been silent in sorrow.

The Ministry of Presence

During that season, I came to understand that God's presence is more powerful than His explanations. He didn't owe me an answer—He offered me Himself.

There were nights when I didn't feel like praying, but I felt His nearness. Days when I didn't have strength to worship, but I sensed His comfort. I realized that even in death, God had not abandoned us. He had simply shifted how He showed up.

Psalm 23 became more than a familiar passage—it became my lifeline.

"Yea, though I walk through the valley of the shadow of death, I will fear no evil: for Thou art with me."

That verse reminded me that faith doesn't remove the valley—it gives you courage to walk through it.

Faith That Grows in the Dark

I used to think faith was proven in victory. But now I know it's also proven in loss. Real faith grows in the dark places where you can't see but still choose to trust.

I began to notice that my faith wasn't weaker after losing my mother—it was deeper. It wasn't about expecting God to prevent pain anymore; it was about believing He could use it.

There's something sacred about realizing that faith isn't about controlling outcomes—it's about surrendering them. It's saying, "God, even if You don't change this, I still choose You."

When you reach that point, grief turns into worship—not because you're happy, but because you've decided that your pain will not silence your praise.

Finding God in the Unanswered

As time went on, I stopped needing every prayer to make sense. I stopped asking God to explain and started asking Him to sustain. And that's when my healing truly began.

Faith doesn't erase the ache, but it gives it meaning. It allows you to see death not as an end, but as a doorway. It helps you remember that the same God who welcomed my mother home is the same One walking with me now.

And when I look back, I see that God never left me—not for a moment. Even in the middle of the funeral, when my heart was breaking, His grace was holding me together.

Faith didn't take away the pain—it transformed it.

✿ Reflection for the Reader

- Have you ever struggled to trust God when His answer wasn't what you prayed for?

- What does "faith in the middle of the funeral" look like for you?

- Take a quiet moment to release your questions to God and invite His peace to take their place.

Prayer:

Father, when life doesn't make sense, help me to trust that You still have a plan. Strengthen my faith when my heart is weak. Teach me to believe not because of what You do, but because of who You are. Even in loss, help me see the life You're still breathing into me. In Jesus' name, amen.

CHAPTER 8

THE HEALING PROCESS — FROM FUNCTIONING TO FEELING

Healing doesn't begin when the tears stop. It begins when you finally give yourself permission to cry.

For a long time, I confused functioning with healing. I was busy, productive, even effective—but not whole. I could organize, serve, and encourage others, yet inside, I was still numb. The ache was buried deep, covered under layers of responsibility, ministry, and family needs.

It's easy to convince yourself that you're healed when life looks put together. But the truth is, busyness can be a bandage too.

There came a moment when God gently interrupted my motion with stillness.

When Survival Becomes a Habit

I remember one morning sitting at my desk, staring at a list of tasks, and realizing I didn't feel anything. Not sadness, not joy—just emptiness. My heart had grown accustomed to survival. I didn't even know what peace felt like anymore.

It was then that I heard a quiet voice in my spirit:

"You've learned how to function, but you've forgotten how to feel."

That truth pierced me. I had spent so much time holding everyone else up that I didn't realize how disconnected I had become from my own soul. I was alive, but not fully living. I was moving, but not healing.

God wasn't calling me to stop functioning; He was calling me to start feeling.

He wanted me to bring my heart back to Him—unfiltered, unguarded, unedited.

The Risk of Feeling Again

Feeling again is frightening when pain has been your companion for so long. You fear that opening your heart will unleash everything you've tried to contain. But God doesn't ask you to feel everything at once—He simply asks you to stop running from what He wants to heal.

So I began to let the emotions surface. Some days, it came in waves— grief, guilt, regret, longing. But alongside those came something else: peace, comfort, and moments of unexpected joy.

It was as if every tear washed away another layer of numbness.

I started journaling again—pouring out prayers I couldn't speak aloud. I began walking outside, feeling the sun, listening to the birds, realizing that life had kept moving even when my heart had paused.

Each small act of openness became an act of healing.

Healing Is Not Linear

There were days I felt like I had made progress—strong, grounded, at peace—and then suddenly, a memory or song would send me spiraling back into sadness. I used to think that meant I was regressing. Now I understand—it meant I was still human.

Healing is not a straight path; it's a sacred cycle of release and renewal. You revisit your pain not because you're stuck, but because God is showing you new layers to surrender.

Some wounds take time—not because God is slow, but because He heals deeply. He's not interested in surface-level recovery; He wants restoration from the inside out.

Letting God Into the Hidden Places

There were corners of my heart I didn't want God to touch. Places filled with "what ifs," with guilt over things I could not change, with questions I couldn't answer. But the Holy Spirit began to nudge me:

"Let Me in there."

It was uncomfortable at first. But I began to see that God doesn't expose pain to shame us—He exposes it to free us.

So I let Him in—into the disappointment, the anger, the loneliness. I stopped pretending to be fine in prayer. I started praying honestly:

"God, I'm tired."

"God, I miss her."

"God, I don't understand, but I still trust You."

And every time I told Him the truth, I felt lighter.

Healing wasn't instant, but it was intentional. Every moment of honesty became an invitation for God to do what I could not do for myself.

Rediscovering Joy

The first time I laughed—really laughed—after my mother's passing, it startled me. For a moment, I felt guilty. How could I laugh when she was gone? But then the Holy Spirit whispered, "This too is healing."

Grief makes you believe that joy is betrayal. Healing teaches you that joy is survival.

I started to give myself permission to smile again, to dream again, to live again. The emptiness began to fade, and in its place grew gratitude—not because the pain was gone, but because I could finally breathe through it.

Joy didn't erase my loss; it reminded me that love had left something eternal behind.

Functioning vs. Feeling

I used to think strength meant not breaking down. Now I know strength means allowing yourself to feel—to embrace both the pain and the promise. Functioning keeps you moving, but feeling keeps you human.

When you allow yourself to feel, you give God something to heal.

And that's where I found my freedom—not in pretending I was over it, but in letting God meet me in it.

❁ Reflection for the Reader

- Have you been functioning instead of feeling?

- What emotions have you buried beneath your responsibilities or faith?

- Ask God to help you release what you've been holding.

Prayer:

Father, I've learned how to keep going, but I need You to teach me how to truly live again. Help me to stop hiding behind strength and start walking in healing. Touch the parts of me I've buried and breathe new life into my heart. Let peace and joy rise again within me. In Jesus' name, amen.

CHAPTER 9

―――――●―――――⌒⌒―――――●―――――

LEADING WITH SCARS

There's a quiet power that comes from scars. They don't bleed anymore, but they never let you forget what you've overcome.

For a long time, I was ashamed of my scars — the emotional ones that came from loving, losing, and leading through pain. But God began to show me that scars are not symbols of weakness; they're evidence of healing. They remind you that what once hurt you no longer has the power to break you.

As I walked through my own healing, I started to lead differently. My voice softened, my perspective deepened, and my compassion expanded. I stopped striving to appear unshakable and started leading from authenticity.

Because the truth is, people don't follow perfection — they follow honesty.

When Leadership Meets Vulnerability

In the early days after my mother's passing, I thought leadership meant maintaining composure at all costs. But now I know that real leadership is not about hiding your pain — it's about using it.

When you've bled in private and healed through God's grace, your presence carries a certain weight. You begin to lead not from theory, but from testimony.

I started to share bits of my story — carefully at first, then more openly. And each time I did, someone would come up and say, "I thought I was the only one." That's when I realized my transparency was a bridge. My scars were creating safe spaces for others to reveal their own.

Vulnerability doesn't diminish leadership — it deepens it. It reminds people that strength is not about being untouchable, but about being human and still trusting God anyway.

The Strength of Softness

Before my loss, I equated strength with toughness — the ability to push through, keep order, and stay composed. But grief softened me. It stripped away my need to control and taught me how to feel again.

I discovered that soft doesn't mean weak. Jesus Himself wept, and yet He changed the world. His tears didn't make Him less divine — they made Him relatable.

Leading with scars means leading with tenderness. It means you can see pain in someone's eyes before they ever speak. It means you stop demanding perfection from others because you remember how it felt to fall apart and still be loved by God.

This new kind of strength isn't loud or showy. It's quiet, steady, and grounded in peace. It's the kind of strength that comes from knowing Who carries you — not how strong you can carry yourself.

From Pressure to Presence

Grief had once made me feel pressured — to stay strong, to lead well, to never show weakness. But now, leadership feels different. It's no longer about performance; it's about presence.

When I walk into a room, I don't need to have all the answers. I've learned that sometimes, the greatest thing you can offer is simply to be there. To listen. To pray. To understand.

My presence carries a different kind of authority now — not the authority of control, but the authority of compassion.

When you've been broken and rebuilt by God, you lead with a peace that surpasses understanding. You stop needing to prove yourself because you know who you are in Him.

Scars That Speak

Every scar has a story, and every story has the power to heal.

When I think about my journey, I no longer see failure or weakness — I see faithfulness. I see how God took shattered pieces and turned them into testimony. I see how He used my pain to produce purpose.

Now, when I speak about grief, I don't speak from a place of sadness but from a place of victory. I can say with confidence: "I've been through the fire, but I didn't burn. I've been broken, but I'm still standing. I've bled, but I didn't drip."

That's the power of a scar — it says, "I survived."

The Beauty of Imperfect Leadership

Leading with scars also means leading without shame. It means knowing that perfection was never the goal — authenticity was.

I don't hide my story anymore. I tell it, not for sympathy, but for strength. Because when others see that you've made it through, they begin to believe that they can too.

The best leaders aren't the ones who never fall; they're the ones who rise and bring others with them. They lead not by pretending to have it all together, but by showing how grace holds them together when life falls apart.

Grace in Every Scar

As I look back now, I see that my scars have become sacred. Each one marks a moment when God met me in my weakness and gave me strength. Each one reminds me of a time when I thought I couldn't make it — and He carried me through.

Scars are not the end of your story; they're the evidence that healing happened. They prove that even in the bleeding, God was working.

So I lead differently now — with humility, with empathy, with peace. I don't strive to be flawless; I strive to be faithful.

Because true leadership isn't about being untouched by pain. It's about walking through it and still pointing others to the One who heals.

❧ Reflection for the Reader

- What scars has God healed that you've been afraid to show?

- How could your story of survival give someone else the courage to heal?

- Ask God to show you how your wounds can speak life to others.

Prayer:

Father, thank You for the strength that comes through my scars. Help me to lead from a place of honesty and grace. Remind me that my imperfections don't disqualify me—they connect me to others. Let every healed wound become a testimony of Your goodness. In Jesus' name, amen.

CHAPTER 10

LIVING AGAIN WITHOUT DRIPPING

There comes a moment in every healing journey when you look around and realize—you're not in the same place you once were. The ache isn't gone, but it's quieter now. The tears still fall sometimes, but they no longer drown you. The memories still come, but they don't crush you.

You're breathing again. Laughing again. Living again.

I used to think healing meant I'd forget my mother, or that I'd reach a place where her absence no longer hurt. But healing doesn't erase memory—it redeems it. It takes the sting and replaces it with strength.

Now when I think of her, I don't only feel pain; I feel gratitude. Gratitude that I got to love someone so deeply that losing her changed me forever.

I can finally say, with peace in my heart: I'm living again—without dripping.

What It Means to "Not Drip"

"Not dripping" doesn't mean you're never moved by emotion. It means you've learned how to manage the flow. You've found balance between remembering and reliving, between feeling and falling apart.

It means you no longer bleed on people who didn't cut you. You've learned how to love without leaking, how to give without depletion, and how to carry your story without collapsing under it.

I used to think strength meant silence. Now I know it means stability—being grounded enough in God's peace that even when emotions rise, they don't overflow uncontrollably.

When you heal, you still feel—but you don't drown.

The Gift of Peace

Peace is not the absence of pain; it's the presence of God in the midst of it.

I remember waking up one morning months after my mother's passing and realizing that my first thought wasn't sorrow. It was gratitude. I smiled—something simple, but powerful. I realized then that peace had quietly taken residence where pain once lived.

That peace didn't come overnight. It came from surrender—daily, sometimes hourly. It came from choosing to trust God's timing even when I didn't understand His methods. It came from letting go of control and allowing Him to rebuild me piece by piece.

And somewhere in the midst of that process, I found my peace again—not the kind the world gives, but the kind Jesus promised in John 14:27:

"Peace I leave with you; my peace I give unto you. I do not give to you as the world gives."

This peace became my foundation. It steadied me when waves of emotion tried to pull me under. It became the quiet assurance that even when life changes, God's love remains constant.

Learning to Love Again

Grief can make you guard your heart. It teaches you how fragile love is, how easily it can be lost. But God began to teach me that love isn't meant to be feared—it's meant to be lived.

I started opening myself again—to connection, to joy, to laughter. I stopped apologizing for enjoying life. Because living doesn't dishonor the one you've lost—it honors them.

My mother loved life. She believed in hope, laughter, and faith even in hardship. So living again became my way of continuing her legacy.

Love didn't die when she did—it just transformed. It became the thread that wove her memory into my purpose.

Purpose Beyond Pain

When grief becomes purpose, your life begins to bloom again. What once broke you becomes what builds you. You start to see how every tear watered something greater inside you—faith, compassion, empathy, resilience.

I found myself ministering differently, leading differently, even worshiping differently. Everything carried new meaning.

Pain had stripped away pretense and left only what was real—God's presence, God's faithfulness, God's grace.

Through it all, I discovered that God doesn't just want us to survive our pain—He wants us to thrive beyond it.

The very thing that wounded me became the very thing God used to awaken my purpose. My grief became a message of healing. My tears became oil for ministry. My scars became signs of grace.

The Freedom of Forgiveness and Surrender

Living again means releasing what no longer serves you—regret, guilt, resentment. It means forgiving those who didn't understand your pain and forgiving yourself for how you handled it.

I had to forgive myself for not grieving "right," for being too strong, too quiet, too busy. But grief has no right or wrong way—it just is. And grace meets you wherever you are.

Surrender became my anthem. I stopped trying to rewrite what had already happened and started asking God to write something beautiful with what remained.

And He did.

Joy That Doesn't Leak

There's a kind of joy that can't be explained. It doesn't come from circumstances; it comes from restoration. It's the joy that sneaks up on you while you're washing dishes, or driving, or sitting in church—and suddenly, you feel whole again.

That's when you know you're healed. When joy returns, not as an emotion, but as an identity.

You're no longer a victim of what happened; you're a vessel of what God did through it.

You're living proof that grief doesn't have the final word—grace does.

A Heart That Still Remembers

Even now, I still miss her. There are moments when I wish I could hear her voice, feel her hand, or sit across from her one more time. But I've learned that memory doesn't have to hurt; it can heal.

I carry her in every prayer I pray, every word I write, every life I touch. Her love didn't end—it expanded. It lives on through me, through every act of kindness, every word of encouragement, every moment of faith.

The void left by her absence has become a vessel for God's presence.

❄ Reflection for the Reader

- What would "living again" look like for you?

- Have you been afraid to feel joy after loss?

- Take a moment to thank God for how far you've come — not because the pain is gone, but because you survived it.

Prayer:

Father, thank You for the gift of new life after loss. Thank You for teaching me that healing doesn't mean forgetting—it means remembering with peace. Help me to live with joy, love deeply, and lead boldly. Let my life be a reflection of Your grace, a testimony that even after bleeding, we can live again—whole, restored, and without dripping. In Jesus' name, amen.

EPILOGUE

THE MINISTRY OF WHOLENESS

When I look back on this journey—from bleeding to healing—I see God's fingerprints everywhere.

He turned my grief into grace, my pain into purpose, and my tears into testimony.

Now, I no longer fear brokenness. I honor it. Because it was in my brokenness that I found God most near.

To anyone reading this who feels like they're still bleeding: hold on. Healing will come. You may not stop feeling the loss, but one day you'll stop drowning in it.

And when that day comes, you'll realize—you are living again.

Not as who you were, but as who you've become through His love.

REFERENCES & SCRIPTURE INDEX

Biblical References

Psalm 34:18 (KJV) — "The Lord is nigh unto them that are of a broken heart; and saveth such as be of a contrite spirit." Referenced in Ch. 1 & 2 to describe God's closeness in seasons of grief.

Romans 8:28 (KJV) — "And we know that all things work together for good to them that love God, to them who are the called according to His purpose." Featured in Ch. 5, illustrating how God redeems suffering and turns pain into purpose.

Romans 12:2 (KJV) — "Be not conformed to this world: but be ye transformed by the renewing of your mind..." Mentioned throughout as a guiding truth for emotional and spiritual transformation in grief.

Psalm 23:4 (KJV) — "Yea, though I walk through the valley of the shadow of death, I will fear no evil: for Thou art with me." Quoted in Ch. 7, emphasizing faith in the darkest places.

John 14:27 (KJV) — "Peace I leave with you, My peace I give unto you..." Central verse in Ch. 10, symbolizing the peace that comes through Christ during healing.

1 Peter 5:7 (KJV) — "Casting all your care upon Him; for He careth for you." Found in Ch. 4, encouraging surrender and emotional honesty with God.

Isaiah 61:3 (KJV) — "To appoint unto them that mourn in Zion, to give unto them beauty for ashes..."

Theme verse for the book's message — that beauty and purpose rise out of pain.

Philippians 4:6–7 (KJV) — "Be careful for nothing; but in every thing by prayer and supplication with thanksgiving let your requests be made known unto God..."

Used in Ch. 8 & 10 to highlight the power of prayer in the healing process.

2 Corinthians 12:9 (KJV) — "My grace is sufficient for thee: for my strength is made perfect in weakness."

Referenced in Ch. 9, revealing that leadership born from brokenness reflects God's true strength.

Matthew 11:28 (KJV) — "Come unto Me, all ye that labour and are heavy laden, and I will give you rest."

Supporting scripture for Ch. 8, encouraging rest in God's care.

Inspirational & Thematic Sources

Granger E. Westberg. Good Grief. Augsburg Books, 2011.

Insightful perspective on the stages of grief and emotional recovery.

Elisabeth Kübler-Ross & David Kessler. On Grief and Grieving. Scribner, 2005.

A psychological framework that parallels the spiritual healing described in this book.

C.S. Lewis. A Grief Observed. HarperOne, 2009.

Candid reflections on faith and loss, resonating with the raw honesty expressed in these chapters.

Joyce Meyer. Healing the Soul of a Woman. FaithWords, 2018.

Spiritual encouragement for emotional restoration and personal wholeness.

T.D. Jakes. When Women Pray. FaithWords, 2020.

Inspirational teachings on prayer and emotional renewal used to support the author's reflections.

Additional Reading for Healing & Growth

The Bible — King James Version (KJV).

The foundation and spiritual compass for every chapter in this work.

Emotionally Healthy Spirituality by Peter Scazzero — Zondervan, 2017.

Guidance on integrating emotional honesty with spiritual maturity.

Boundaries by Dr. Henry Cloud and Dr. John Townsend — Zondervan, 2017.

Principles that reinforce the importance of emotional and spiritual boundaries while healing.

PROPHET DR. LARON MATTHEWS, PH.D.

A Man of Integrity, Vision, and Prophetic Insight

Prophet Dr. Laron Matthews, Ph.D., is a distinguished man of God whose ministry is marked by integrity, divine wisdom, and prophetic accuracy. A gifted communicator and visionary leader, he bridges generations by uniting the young and the seasoned in faith, purpose, and spiritual maturity. His life and ministry reflect the unity expressed in John 17:22 and the wisdom found in Proverbs 17:27, making him a respected and relevant voice in the 21st-century Church.

Born on October 31, 1967, Prophet Matthews is the seventh of eighteen children born to Bishop Nathaniel and the late Mrs. Suzanne Matthews. Raised in an environment rooted in holiness, faith, and service, he developed a deep commitment to ministry at an early age. He is a devoted father and grandfather whose leadership reflects strong Christian family values and the legacy of prayer and love passed down from his late mother.

Prophet Matthews attended Joliet Township High School Central, Joliet Junior College, and The Economic Business Institute, where he developed administrative and business principles that support his ministry leadership. He was licensed to preach the Gospel in February 1996 and later ordained in July 1997 under the late Bishop George King. In February 2001, he received Apostolic Prophetic Impartation into the Ascension Office of the Prophet, and in September 2006, he was ordained to the Pastoral Office. Throughout his ministry, he has served in key leadership roles, including financial oversight, youth leadership, and ministry protocol training.

He currently serves as **Senior Pastor of Restoration Foundation Prophetic International Ministries** in Harvey, Illinois, and oversees **Restoration Destiny Center** in San Antonio, Texas. He is also the founder of **Laron Matthews Ministries**, headquartered in Montgomery, Alabama, through which he equips leaders, strengthens believers, and advances prophetic understanding globally. Prophet Matthews hosts Prophetic Explosion Crusades and Conferences nationwide, emphasizing revelation, healing, and the manifestation of God's power.

In addition to ministry, Prophet Matthews has made a meaningful civic impact. He founded the Inner-City Counselors and Training Program for the Joliet Park District and served on the Will County Gang Task Force, working with community leaders to promote peace, restoration, and family stability.

Academically, Prophet Matthews earned a Bachelor's Degree in Ministry and a Master's Degree in Christian Counseling from American Bible University and is licensed through the New Covenant Christian Counselors Association. He received an Honorary Doctorate in 2017 and earned his Doctor of Philosophy (Ph.D.) in Christian Education in 2018 from Global Evangelical Christian College and

Seminary. He is the author of *Love: The Unfinished Chapter, Love: The Unfinished Chapter—What Should've Been Told*, and *The Encounter with Wisdom: The Secret of Her*, works that reflect his prophetic insight and passion for healing and truth.

Prophet Matthews' ministry has been recognized with numerous honors, including the **Lifetime Presidential Award** and **Author of the Year 2025**. Anchored in Isaiah 6:8, his life's mission is to answer God's call with obedience and compassion, advancing the Kingdom, restoring families, and uniting believers through faith and revelation.

Sunday Service: 7:30 a.m. CST – Facebook Live (Laron Matthews)

Conference Line: 218-548-3684 | Passcode: 435160#

Theme Scriptures: John 17:22 • Proverbs 17:27 • Proverbs 18:24 • Isaiah 6:8

Booking Information

If you would like to invite **Dr. Laron Matthews** to speak at your church, conference, or event:

Phone: 877-912-2027

Website: www.werestoreu.org

Facebook: *Laron Matthews*

www.ingramcontent.com/pod-product-compliance
Lightning Source LLC
Chambersburg PA
CBHW070134100426
42744CB00009B/1832